Witches in the Kitchen
Delicious Recipes for the Eight Sabbats

By Roc Marten

PDP Publications

Copyright 2011 PDP Publications

PDP Publications

http://www.pdppublications.com

TABLE of CONTENTS

IMBOLC

Imbolc, also known as Candlemass, occurs six weeks after Yule and six weeks before the Spring Equinox. During this time Wiccans honor the Celtic Triple Goddess, Brid.

Traditional foods used during Imbolc come from a variety of dairy products and are spiced with garlic, shallots, leeks, onions and/or olives.

Swedish Waffles

3 Eggs

1 tsp. granulated sugar

1 cup evaporated milk or cream

1/4 cup melted butter

1-1/2+ cup flour

2 tsp. baking powder

1/4 tsp. salt

Preheat waffle iron. Combine all of the ingredients in a large mixing bowl and mix until the ingredients begin to have a slightly puffy appearance.

Pour the mixture into the waffle iron and bake until done.

Top off the Waffle with preserves or honey, as is the Swedish tradition. You may substitute the preserves and honey with butter or whipped cream as they are suitable dairy products.

4

Asparagus Spears with Herb Sauce

2 Tbl. margarine or butter

2 Tbl. flour

1/4 tsp. salt

1/6 tsp. pepper

1 tsp. dill

dash sage

dash nutmeg

1 cup milk

Melt margarine over a low heat until completely melted. Stir in salt, flour, dill, pepper, nutmeg and sage. Cook over medium heat, stirring constantly; remove from heat when mixture is smooth. Stir in milk. Heat to boiling, stirring constantly for 1 minute. Pour sauce over Asparagus spears when ready to serve.

Curried Lamb with Barley

2 Tbs. butter or oil

1 onion, chopped

1 1/2 lbs. lean lamb, sliced into thin strips

1 C. beef or vegetable broth

1/2 C. barley

2 Tbs. curry powder

1/2 C. golden raisins

In a large skillet, heat the oil or butter. Sautee the onion until it is soft, add the strips of lamb. Brown the lamb, but not so long that the lamb gets tough – the goal here is to keep it nice and tender. Slowly pour in the broth.

Add the barley, cover the pan. Allow to simmer for about 20 minutes, or until the barley has cooked. Uncover the pan, and add curry and raisins. Simmer for an additional few minutes, remove from heat.

Boiled Custard

1 quart milk

4 large eggs

1/4 tsp. Salt

3/4 cup sugar

1 tsp. Vanilla

Scald milk in a heavy pan. DO NOT BOIL! Thoroughly beat eggs, adding sugar and salt. Beat a small portion of the scalded milk into the egg mixture, stirring constantly.

Pour the egg mixture onto the scalded milk, stirring well. Slowly bring to a boil until the mixture coats a wooden spoon.

Remove from heat and beat until cool.

Add vanilla and chill.

OSTARA

Ostara is celebrated at the Vernal Equinox, the first day of Spring. The Teutonic Goddess of Fertility is in her aspect of mother to be.

Traditional foods play a part in this holiday such as eggs, meats and vegetables.

Queens Biscuits

4 cups Flour, sifted

1 cup Sugar

1 Tablespoon Baking powder

1/4 teaspoon Salt

1 cup Shortening

2 Eggs, slightly beaten

1/2 cup Milk

1/4 pound Sesame seeds

Lightly grease 2 cookie sheets. In a bowl, sift together the flour, sugar, baking powder and salt.

Cut in with pastry blender or two knives until pieces are size of small peas. Add shortening and stir in eggs and milk. Make a soft dough. Mix thoroughly together. Break dough into small pieces and roll each piece between the palms of your hands to form rolls that measure about 1-1/2-" in length. Flatten rolls slightly, and roll in sesame seeds. Place on cookie sheets about 3" apart. Bake at 375~ for 12-15 minutes or until cookies are lightly browned. Makes 6 dozen cookies.

Rosemary Potatoes

1 1/2 pounds small potatoes

2 Tablespoons Olive oil

1/2 teaspoon Salt

2 cloves garlic, minced

1 1/2 Tablespoons Fresh rosemary, chopped

Cover the potatoes with water and bring to a simmer. Cooking for 5 minutes. Drain and toss the potatoes into a pan. Place the pan over heat until the outside of the potatoes are dry. Add olive oil, salt, garlic, and fresh rosemary. Place the potatoes into a baking pan, in one layer, and bake in a 350~ oven until crispy and browned, about 15-20 minutes.

Ardshane House Irish Stew

4 pounds Middle neck of Lamb, cut into 1" cubes

4 pounds Potatoes, peeled and cubed

10 small Onions, quartered

2 ounces Pearl Barley

2 pints Stock

Salt and Pepper to taste

There are several variations to this recipe however I am presenting you with the basic recipe for this meal.

In a large kettle add 10 cups of water. Place all ingredients in kettle, bring to a boil. After bringing to a boil, lower your heat, and allow to simmer for about two hours. If you need more water, add as you see fit. Add salt & pepper for seasoning.

Honey and Orange Tea Loaf

6 ounces Self Rising flour

6 ounces Honey

1 ounce Margarine

1 large Egg

1 teaspoon Baking Powder

6 Tablespoons Milk

1 large Orange, grated rind

Preheat oven to 350 degrees F. Grease and line a 2 lb. loaf tin or pan. Cream the margarine and honey together in a bowl, mixing thoroughly. Add egg and beat vigorously. Sieve the flour, salt and baking powder and add alternately with the milk, to the creamed mixture. Sprinkle in the orange rind and mix well.

Spoon the mixture into the tin. Bake for 45 minutes. Remove from the oven, glaze with honey and return to the oven for an additional 10 minutes. Remove from the tin or pan and cool.

Serve sliced and buttered.

BELTANE

Beltane, also known as Roodmass, is celebrated on May 1st. Translated, Beltane means "Bright Fire".

Foods used in celebration of Beltane include, vegetables, herbs and meats.

Donnegal Oatmeal Cream

15 fluid ounces Milk

1/2 cup Medium oatmeal - cracked, not rolled

1 Large egg (beaten)

rind & juice of 1 orange

2 teaspoons Sugar (to taste)

1/2 ounce Gelatin

2 Tablespoons Water

8 ounces Heavy cream, whipped

Fruit sauce of choice

Soak the oatmeal in milk for 30 minutes. Pour into a pan, place over heat and bring to a boil, stirring constantly. Let simmer for 3 to 4 minutes. Pour mixture into a bowl and add the beaten egg, grated lemon rind, and sugar to taste. Dissolve the gelatin in the orange juice and water, add to the mixture once it's cooled, and then fold in the cream. Pour the entire mixture into a glass bowl and leave to set. Serve with your favorite fruit sauce on top.

Asparagus with Chives and Blossoms

1 pound Asparagus, washed

1 Tablespoon Olive oil

1 Tablespoon Sesame Seeds

2 Tablespoons Fresh Chives, snipped

16 Chive Blossoms

1/2 teaspoon Soy Sauce

Salt & Pepper for taste

Blanch the asparagus in lightly salted boiling water for about 3 minutes or until tender/crisp; it is important that you do not overcook. Run asparagus under very cold water and drain. Remove the chive stalks to separate the flowers.

In a skillet, heat the oil over medium heat and add the sesame seed. Stir for 1 minute, add the snipped chives, and stir for an additional. Add the asparagus and soy sauce to the skillet with a few pinches of salt and generous amount of pepper; stir well, cover, and cook for few a minutes. Remove the lid, sprinkle the chive blooms over the asparagus, and cover for 1 to 2 minutes so that the chive blooms steam briefly.

Stir lightly. Serve hot.

Chicken Barley Stew with Herbs

2-3 LB chicken breasts on the bone

2 Tablespoons Butter

1 LB leeks (3-4 large ones, 4-5 little ones) thickly cut. May substitute onions

4 cloves garlic, chopped fine

6 oz barley

3 Tablespoons red wine vinegar

3 3/4 cups water

2 bay leaves

1 Tablespoon dried sage

Melt the butter, then fry the leeks and garlic in the butter. Add the chicken to the leeks and garlic and brown. Add remaining ingredients, reserving the sage. Bring to a boil, then reduce and simmer for 1 to 1-1/2 hours. Remove chicken from pot and let cool. Remove meat from bones and add back to the pot. Add sage. Stir well and serve.

Oatcakes

1/2 cup Shortening

1 cup Oats or quick-cooking oats

1 cup All-purpose flour

1/2 teaspoon Baking soda

1/4 teaspoon Salt

2 - 3 Tablespoons Cold Water

Cut shortening into four ingredients until mixture resembles fine crumbs. Add water, 1 Tablespoon at a time, until it forms a stiff dough. Roll until 1/8 inch thick on lightly floured surface. Cut into 2 inch rounds or squares. Place on cookie sheet and bake at 375 degrees until they begin to brown – normally takes 12 to 15 minutes.

SUMMER SOLSTICE

Litha is the celebration of the summer solstice.

Summer crops such as fruits and vegetables are the preferred food choice to help celebrate Summer Solstice.

Fresh Fruit Fennel Salad

1 large fennel bulbs

2 fresh oranges

    1 apple

    3 green onions

    1/4 C. water

    3 Tbs. balsamic vinegar

    2 Tbs. olive oil

    2 Tbs. honey mustard

    1 Tbs. chopped fresh rosemary

Shave the fennel into thin pieces, and toss it into a large bowl. Peel and divide the oranges, and chunk up the apple, dice the green onions, and add all these to the fennel.

Combine the water, olive oil, balsamic vinegar, rosemary, honey mustard and garlic in a bowl and whisk until blended. Drizzle over the fennel and fruit salad.

Grilled Vegetables

4 bell peppers

2 onions

2 yellow squash

4 Portobello mushrooms

2 zucchini

A bunch of green onions

1/2 pound asparagus spears, trimmed

Olive oil

Salt and pepper

Balsamic vinegar to taste

3 cloves garlic, minced

Fresh rosemary

Oregano

Preheat a grilling pan over medium heat. Trim and wash all the vegetables. Cut the larger vegetables into slices. Put the vegetables in a bowl and drizzle olive oil on them. Shake the bowl so all the vegetables become lightly coated with olive oil. Sprinkle with salt and pepper for additional flavor.

Add the vegetables to the grilling pan, and grill them until they are tender. They should be lightly charred, which will take anywhere from 8 - 12 minutes.

While the vegetables are grilling, combine 1/4 Cup of olive oil with the balsamic vinegar, rosemary, garlic and oregano. Remove the veggies from the grill, place them in a bowl, and then add the herb and oil mix. Toss to coat them with the herb and oil mix.

Fiery Grilled Salmon

2 lbs salmon fillets, skin on

1/4 C. soy sauce

   1/4 C. Dijon mustard

Combine the olive oil, Dijon mustard, soy sauce garlic and cayenne pepper in a bowl and whisk together. Using a barbeque brush, brush half of the soy sauce mix onto the salmon fillets. Place them sauce-side down on the grill for about six to seven minutes. Brush the remainder of the sauce onto the skin side, and use a large spatula to flip the fillets over. Grill for another five minutes and remove from heat.

Candied Ginger

1 lb ginger root

   3 Cups white sugar, divided

2 Cups water

   1/2 Cup white corn syrup

 Peel the skin from the ginger root and chop into small pieces. Combine 2 cups of sugar, water and corn syrup in a crock pot and bring to high heat, stirring occasionally. Once the sugar has melted, add the ginger to the liquid. Cover, reduce heat, and allow to simmer, for 12 hours.

After the ginger has simmered for 12 hours, drain off the liquid. Place ginger in a bowl with the remaining 1 cup of sugar, and toss so that it becomes completely coated. Pour on a sheet of wax paper to cool.

LAMMAS

Lammas falls at the beginning of harvest season. Lammas is a time of excitement and magic, when the natural world is thriving around us.

Preferred food to celebrate Lammas would include, anything from the garden and poultry make fine meals to celebrate this Wiccan tradition.

Potato Griddle Cakes

1 cup hot unseasoned mashed potatoes

2 tablespoons butter or margarine, softened

2 eggs, beaten

1 cup grated unpeeled raw potatoes

1/2 cup flour

2 teaspoons baking powder

1 teaspoon salt

1 teaspoon caraway seeds (optional)

1/4 teaspoon pepper

1/4 cup milk

In large bowl mix together the mashed potatoes and
2 tablespoons butter. Stir in grated potatoes, eggs, flour, baking
powder, salt, caraway seeds and pepper. Add the milk. Heat
1tablespoon of butter to sizzling in large nonstick skillet. Drop
potato mixture,
about 2 1/2 tablespoons at a time, into skillet, flattening slightly to
form patties. Cook over medium-high heat until crisp and
browned, turning once.

Repeat with remaining potato mixture, adding butter to skillet as needed.

Beef Tenderloin with Blackberry Port Wine

Beef Tenderloins

1 large shallot or small onion, finely diced

1 cup fresh or frozen blackberries, divided

2 cups port wine 1 tsp. sugar

2 cups beef stock

1 Tbsp. butter, softened

In a saucepan bring the diced shallot, 3/4 cup blackberries, wine and sugar to a boil. Strain and set liquid aside.

Taking about 15 minutes, Boil beef stock in a separate pan to reduce by half.

Grill tenderloins in a skillet 3-4 minutes per side. Whisk blackberry and port wine into beef stock.

Brown Rice with Pine Nuts

1 1/2 cups Long-Grain Brown Rice

3 cups Water

1 medium Onion, chopped

2 Tablespoons Vegetable Oil

1 Tablespoon Ground Cumin

Black Pepper, to taste

1 Tablespoon Fresh Parsley, minced

1/4 cup Pine Nuts

Soak the brown rice in water for at least 2 hours. Heat oil in a heavy skillet with a tight-fitting lid. Add chopped onion and sauté the onions until golden brown and limp. Add rice and soaking water along with cumin and pepper. Bring to a boil, reduce heat, and cover. Cook at a simmer for about 20 minutes. Rice should be tender and water should be absorbed. When rice is done, add chopped parsley and pine nuts.

Rich Whiskey Shortbread

4 oz Butter

1 1/2 tbl Single malt scotch whiskey

3 oz Caster (granulated) sugar

1 1/2 oz Almonds; blanched

1 oz Mixed peel; chopped

6 oz Plain (all-purpose) flour

2 oz Rice flour

Cut the butter into small pieces.

Place in a bowl together with a tablespoon of whiskey and the sugar.

Cream the mixture until fluffy.

Finely chop two-thirds of the almonds and add to the mixture.

Stir in the peel and the flour.

Draw the mixture together and press into a buttered 8-inch sandwich tin.

Prick well and pinch up the edges decoratively.

Halve the remaining almonds and place these on top of the shortbread.

AUTUMN EQUINOX

Autumnal Equinox, also known as The Harvest Festival, occurs approximately on the 21st of September. The Autumn Equinox is a time to give thanks for the harvest and to clear away the chaff and rubbish, both physically and metaphysically.

Preferred food to celebrate this Harvest Festival would include food made from fresh fall vegetables and fruits.

Apple Butter

4 quarts Apple

2 quarts Water

1 1/2 quarts Cider

1 1/2 pounds Sugar

1 teaspoon Cinnamon

1 teaspoon Allspice

1 teaspoon Cloves

Wash and slice the apples into small bits. Cover with water and boil until soft. Press through a sieve to remove skins and seeds. Bring cider to a boil and then add apple pulp and sugar and cook until it thickens, constantly stirring to prevent scorching. Add spices and cook until it is thick enough for spreading. Pour into sterilized jars and seal.

Cock – a – Leekie Soup

3 1/2 pounds Frying Chicken, cut into 8 pieces

1 pound Beef Shanks, cut into 1" pieces

6 cups Chicken broth

3 slices Thick cut Bacon

1 Tablespoon Dried leaf Thyme

1 Bay leaf

3/4 cup Pearl Barley

1 1/2 cups Chopped Leek, white only

Salt and Pepper to taste

2 Tablespoons Chopped parsley

Place the chicken, beef, bacon, stock, thyme, and bay leaf in a large pot, add water and bring to a boil. Reduce the heat and simmer, covered, for 30 minutes. While simmering, boil the barley in 1 1/2 cups water for 10 minutes. Drain and set aside. Remove chicken from pot, de-bone and set aside. Add leeks and barley to the pot, and simmer 15 minutes. Remove beef shanks and de-bone. Chop meat coarsely, and return to the pot, along with the chicken.

Simmer covered, for 5 minutes more. Season with salt and pepper to taste.

Roast Filet of Beef

1 Fillet of beef (5-6 lb) trimmed

5 Garlic cloves, slivered

1 teaspoon Salt

1 teaspoon Freshly ground pepper

Tabasco sauce

1 cup Soy sauce

1/2 cup Olive oil

1 cup Port wine

2 teaspoons Thyme

1 bunch Watercress

To prepare the fillet, make slits in it and put slivers of garlic in the slits. Rub the filet with salt, pepper and Tabasco. Combine the soy sauce, olive oil, port and herbs in a bowl and place the fillet in this marinade in for about a 1/2 hour unrefrigerated. Turn the filet several times while it is marinating. Preheat oven to 425 degrees.

Roast the filet for 30-35 minutes, basting occasionally with the marinade. After it is removed from the oven, allow the fillet to rest, covered with foil, up to 30 minutes.

After unwrapping the filet cut into slices and place on a warm platter. Garnish with sprigs of watercress.

Pecan Pie

1-1/4 Cups Pecan Pieces

2 Eggs, Slightly Beaten

1 Cup Light Karo Syrup

1/4 Cup Sugar

2 Tablespoons Flour

1/4 Teaspoon Salt

1 Teaspoon Vanilla.

Preheat oven to 375 degrees. Spread the pecans in an unbaked 9-inch pie shell. Mix all of the remaining ingredients together and pour over the pecans.

Place in oven and bake for about 1 hour.

SAMHAIN

Samhain, also known as Eve of all Souls, is celebrated on the 31st of October. To Wiccans, the Samhain Rite is the most important of the year, signifying the death of the old year, and the rebirth of the new year. Christians celebrate this day as Halloween.

Preferred foods used in celebration of this rite includes pumpkins, spices, vegetables and meat.

Pumpkin Bread

2/3 cup Shortening

1 teaspoon Nutmeg

2 2/3 cups Sugar

1 teaspoon Cinnamon

4 large Eggs

2 teaspoons Baking soda

1 teaspoon Vanilla

1/2 teaspoon Baking powder

3 1/3 cups Flour

2/3 cup Water

1 can Pumpkin

1 1/2 teaspoons Salt

Preheat oven to 350 degrees. In a large bowl, mix all of the ingredients together, pour into 2 loaf pans. Bake for 50 - 60 minutes.

Colcannon

4 medium Potatoes, peeled and boiled

3 Tablespoons Butter

1/2 teaspoon Salt

1/8 teaspoon Black Pepper

1/4 cup Milk

2 Tablespoons Sour Cream

8 ounces Kale, steamed and chopped

1 Tablespoon Onion, grated

Mash potatoes with salt, pepper, butter, milk and sour cream until fluffy and light. Stir in grated onion and kale.

Roast Loin of Pork

1 Pork Loin

1 small Onion, chopped

1 cloves Garlic, minced

1 Tablespoon Fresh parsley, chopped

1/2 Bay leaf, crushed

1/2 teaspoon Celery seeds

1/2 teaspoon Dry thyme

4 Whole cloves

1 teaspoon Beef bouillon

Salt & Pepper for flavor

Preheat oven to 300 degrees. Fold 2 large sheets of aluminum foil together creating a double fold, leaving enough space to enclose the pork loin. Place pork loin on foil. Stick cloves into loin and sprinkle all other ingredients over the top. Tightly enclose the pork loin in foil and cook for approximately 45 minutes PER pound.

Irish Apple Fritters

5 ounces Flour

5 fluid ounces Water

1/4 teaspoon Salt

2 each Eggs (separated)

1 tablespoon Melted butter

2 each Large cooking apples

4 ounces Sugar

Lemon juice

Oil for deep frying

Sift flour and salt together. Create a well in the center. Add the cooled melted butter and some of the water and egg yolks. Work in the flour and beat until smooth. Add remaining water. Leave to stand. Just before using, beat the egg whites until stiff but not dry. Fold into batter mix.

Peel, core and slice apples..try to keep the slices about ¼ to ½ inches thick. Dip apples into batter and deep fry until golden. Drain and serve dredged with sugar and sprinkled with lemon juice.

YULE

Yule, The winter Solstice, is celebrated on approximately.

December 22nd. Yule is a traditional day of gathering with loved ones and feasting, the sharing of gifts and thinking about others.

As with other celebrations, preferred foods for Yule celebrations include spices, herbs, dairy and meats.

Ginger Cakes

1 cup Shortening

1 cup Brown sugar

2 each Egg, well beaten

1 cup Molasses

4 cups Flour

1 teaspoon Soda

1 Tablespoon boiling Water

1 teaspoon Ginger

1 pinch Salt

To create your shortening you will use a mixture of lard and butter. Preheat oven to 350 degrees. Cream the sugar and shortening together. Add eggs and beat thoroughly. Add the molasses and baking soda to a pot and bring to a boil. After bringing to a boil pour the molasses and baking soda, which should be dissolved with beaten eggs. Sift the flour and ginger together and combine with the other ingredients. Mix well. Pour into well-greased muffin pans and bake for approximately 20 minutes.

Acorn Squash and Potato Soup

1 large Onion, chopped (1 cup)

1 Tablespoon Vegetable oil

1 1/2 pounds Sweet Potatoes, peeled and cubed (5 cups)

1 small Acorn Squash, seeded and cubed

13 3/4 ounces Chicken Broth

4 Tablespoons Milk

1/2 teaspoon Salt

1/4 teaspoon White Pepper

1/4 cup Sour Cream

2 Tablespoons Sliced Almonds; toasted

Ground Nutmeg

In a large saucepan, sauté the onion in oil over medium heat until onion is golden brown. Add squash, potatoes and broth. Simmer, covered, until vegetables become tender, approximate cook time is 25 minutes.

Roast Loin of Venison with Cranberries

2 thick slices of lemon

2 thick slices of orange

2 slices of peeled fresh ginger

1 1/2 cups sugar

1 small bay leaf

2 cups fresh cranberries

4 pounds boneless loin of venison

2 Tablespoons olive oil

1 teaspoon salt

1 1/4 teaspoons freshly ground pepper

3/4 teaspoon finely chopped juniper berries

2 cups dry red wine

2 cups beef or venison stock

2 Tablespoons cold butter, cut into pieces

Fresh thyme sprigs, for garnish

In a medium nonstick saucepan, combine the orange, lemon, sugar, ginger and bay leaf with 1 cup of cold water. Bring to a boil, stirring to dissolve the sugar. Reduce the heat to moderate temperature and boil, uncovered, until syrupy, this takes approximately10 to 15 minutes.

Add in the cranberries, continuing to stir. Remove from heat and allow to cool. Transfer the mixture to a glass container, cover and refrigerate for 1 to 2 days, stirring once or twice during that time.

Preheat the oven to 400F. Rub the venison with olive oil, 3/4 teaspoon of the salt, ½ teaspoon of chopped juniper berries and 1 teaspoon of the pepper, pressing the seasonings into the meat. Place the loin in a roasting pan and roast, basting frequently with the pan juices. Loosely Cover the venison with foil and set aside for 10 to 15 minutes before carving.

Meanwhile, remove and discard the bay leaf and the lemon, orange and ginger slices from the cranberries. In a food processor or blender, puree half the cranberries and half the liquid until smooth.

In a medium saucepan, boil the wine until reduced to 1/2 cup. Add the stock and bring to a boil. Add the cranberry puree, simmer, uncovered, until slightly thickened. Remove from heat. Strain the remaining whole cranberries and add them to the sauce with the remaining 1/4 teaspoon each of pepper, salt and chopped juniper berries. Swirl in the cold butter.

Yule Log Cookies

1/2 cup Brown sugar, firmly packed

3 Tablespoons Butter or margarine, softened

1 Egg

1 cup All-purpose flour

1/2 teaspoon Baking powder

1/2 teaspoon Ground cardamom

1/4 teaspoon Baking soda

1/4 teaspoon Ground cinnamon

1/4 teaspoon Ground cloves

1/4 teaspoon Ground allspice

1/4 teaspoon Ground nutmeg

Red and green decorator icing

Preheat oven to 375 degrees.

In a bowl, beat the margarine and brown sugar until blended. Add the egg; beating until well blended. Lightly spoon flour into measuring cup. Add the flour, baking soda, baking powder and spices; mix well. Divide the dough in half. On a lightly floured surface, roll each half of dough with your hands to make two 10

1/2-inch logs; flatten slightly to 1 1/4 inches in diameter. With a spatula, place the logs 2 to 3 inches apart on an ungreased cookie sheet. Dip a non-serrated knife in water; score each log diagonally at 3/4-inch intervals. Bake for 11 to 13 minutes, or until set and no longer moist. Allow to cool for 1 minute.

Remove from the cookie sheet; place on a wire rack. Cool for an additional 5 minutes. Cut the logs at the scored lines.

Allow to cool completely. Decorate each cookie using the red and green icing.

COOKING TERMS

Batter ---A mixture of flour, sugar, eggs, milk, etc. which can be poured

Beat---To lift a mixture with a spoon or an electric mixer to inject air and make the mixture smooth and creamy

Blanch---To scald, make white, to partially cook an item, to place fruits or nuts in boiling water to remove the skins, or to dip vegetables in boiling water in preparation for freezing, canning, or drying

Blend---To mix thoroughly two or more ingredients

Boiling point---The temperature reached when a mixture maintains a full bubbling motion on its surface

Boil---To cook in a liquid, generally water, in which large bubbles rise quickly and steadily so that all the liquid is agitated

Bouillon---A liquid similar to a stock, but cleaner and richer in flavor

Braise---To cook meat by searing in fat, then simmering in a covered dish in a small amount of liquid or to brown meat or vegetables in hot fat, then to cook slowly in a small amount of liquid

Breading---To coat an item with a mixture of flour, egg, and bread crumbs

Brew---To cook in hot liquid until the flavor is extracted

Broil ---To cook by exposing the food directly to the heat

Broth---The liquid that meat, fish, poultry, or vegetables have been simmered in

Candying---To cook certain fruits or vegetables in a heavy sweet syrup

Caramelize---To heat granulated sugar to a golden brown color for the purpose of flavoring and coloring other food

Chop---To cut into small pieces using a knife or other sharp utensil

Clarify---To make a liquid clear by adding beaten egg white and egg shells. The egg jells in the hot liquid and cloudiness adheres to it and then the liquid is strained

Coatspoon---When a mixture forms a thin, even film on a spoon

Core ---To remove the central seed part of certain fruits, such as apples or pears

Cream ---To beat until soft and fluffy, generally applies to shortening and sugar

Dice---To cut into small cubes or squares

Dissolve---To cause a dry substance to become fluid or to absorb into liquid

Dough---A thick, soft uncooked mass of moistened flour and other ingredients

Drawn butter---Melted butter

Dredge---To coat an item with dry ingredients such as flour

Dress ---To trim or clean poultry or fish

Fine herbs ---A combination of three or four herbs chopped very fine

Fold---To mix, using a motion beginning vertically down through the mixture, continuing across the bottom of the bowl and ending with an upward and over movement

Fritters---Food dipped or coated with a batter and fried to a golden brown in oil

Garnish---To decorate a dish with an item to improve its look

Glaze---To coat or cover an item with a glossy coating

Grate ---To rub or wear into small particles, by rubbing on the rough surface of a grater

Herbs---Savory leaves such as tarragon, sage, basil, parsley, oregano, etc.

Knead---To place dough on a flat surface and work it, pressing down with your hands, then folding over and over again

Melt---To dissolve or make liquid by heating

Mince ---To cut food into very small, fine pieces such as carrots, onions, and celery

Mixing---To combine two or more ingredients

Pare---To cut off the outer covering or skin with a knife or other sharp tool

Peel---To strip off an outer covering or skin

Poach---To cook in water that bubbles only slightly

Reduce---To concentrate a liquid by simmering for a long time

Roux---A mixture of fat and flour cooked together, usually in equal parts, over low heat until the flour and fat blend together smoothly and is used to thicken soups, sauces, gravies, and stews

Saute---To quickly heat meat or vegetables in fat in an open pan

Scald---To heat milk or cream just below the boiling point until a scum forms on the surface

Scone---A type of Scottish quick bread similar to a biscuit

Sear ---To scorch or char the surface of meat quickly, sealing in the juices

Shred---Cut into thin pieces, using the large holes of a grater or cheese shredder

Simmer---To cook liquid just below the boiling point

Smother---To cook in a covered container until tender or cover an item with another item completely

Stir---To blend ingredients using a circular motion
Stock---The liquid in which meat, poultry, fish, or vegetables have been cooked

Tenderloin---A strip of very tender meat generally referring to beef, pork, lamb, and veal

Zest ---A rind of lemon or orange

Disclaimer: No one involved in the writing of this book or its contents may be held responsible for any adverse reactions arising from following any of the instructions/recipes presented in this book. It is the reader's personal responsibility to exercise all precautions and use his or her own discretion if following any instructions from this book.

PDP Publications

Copyright 2011 PDP Publications

PDP Publications

http://www.pdppublications.info

Printed in Great Britain
by Amazon.co.uk, Ltd.,
Marston Gate.